THE BLUE DEN

Stephanie Norgate is a playwright and poet. She lives in Sussex with her husband and two children, and runs the MA in Creative Writing at the University of Chichester. Her plays have been produced on the London Fringe and her radio plays broadcast on BBC Radio 4. *Fireclay*, a Poetry Business prize-winning pamphlet appeared in 1998, followed by a selection of poems in *Oxford Poets 2000*. Her two collections with Bloodaxe are *Hidden River* (2008), which was shortlisted for both the Forward Prize for Best First Collection and the Jerwood Aldeburgh First Collection Prize, and *The Blue Den* (2012). She is currently editing a book of international essays on poetry and voice.

STEPHANIE NORGATE

THE BLUE DEN

BLOODAXE BOOKS

ISBN: 978 1 85224 937 3

First published in 2012 by
Bloodaxe Books Ltd,
Highgreen,
Tarset,
Northumberland NE48 1RP,

www.bloodaxebooks.com
For further information about Bloodaxe titles
please visit our website or write to
the above address for a catalogue.

Supported using public funding by
ARTS COUNCIL
ENGLAND

Cover design: Neil Astley & Pamela Robertson-Pearce.

Printed in Great Britain by
Bell & Bain Limited, Glasgow, Scotland.

for Francesca and Ben

ACKNOWLEDGEMENTS

Thanks are due to the editors of the following magazines, anthologies and websites where some of these poems first appeared: *The Oxford Magazine, Poetry and Jazz 2010 and 2011, The Poetry Archive, A Track of Light, Magma, MsLexia,* the *Troubadour* website, *Poetry South East, Hippocrates Prize Poetry and Medicine Anthology, This Island City, Writing in Education, Best British Poetry 2012*. The 'Other Voices' poems, written as a result of my collaboration with painter Jayne Sandys-Renton, were originally recorded by actors and broadcast as a sound installation in the Otter Gallery during the exhibition, *The Fallen House and Other Voices*. Many thanks to the other voices: Hannah Burton, Liza Burton, Robert Gould, Francesca Mollett, Ben Mollett, Chloe Salaman, Toby Salaman and to the producers of the CD, Hamish Sandys-Renton and Tim Sandys-Renton. I would like to thank the curators and trustees of the Otter Gallery where I am poet in residence. In the writing of 'Pipe', I especially acknowledge Rachel Cunningham's photographic exhibition *Quiet Transfer* which records fragments of Palestinian houses demolished in East Jerusalem. 'February Fences' and 'Free Style' were commissioned for *The Poets' Calendar 2012* (Chi Poets and University of Chichester – with many thanks to my colleagues).

Thanks to Helen Dunmore and Stephen Mollett for reading work-in-progress. Thanks to Joanna Curtis for the deep relaxation. Thanks to Anne Caldwell for talking about time.

CONTENTS

Other Voices: Stream to Ice

Children wake me to my new voice, that tone
like birdsong, the weak cheeping of a finch.
You have made me an invisible ice bird
whose song rises from pools stalled where they led.
I wasn't expecting this change of being,
this suspension of flow, these notes that stones
chip from our shared surface of rime. You don't flinch
at the scatter of flints, or dry sticks hurled
to strike the sound from us. You have stolen
the dark holly and mirrored its blue green,
stilled us to the shade of a mallard's head.
Even the drizzle of water from the wishing well
has frozen into a splay of ice flowers, swollen,
as coins sink slowly, sunned in your breaking spell.

Plastic Bags Along the A27

They want their lives back,
these pale heads, flip-flapping,
marooned on brambles.

They want back into cars,
back on board ferries, back
into the hands that let them slip

to become these fluttering sails
straining at their moorings,
the red or acid yellow of the dogwood.

In the small harbour
of the lay-by at dusk,
the bags exhale and flop.

But in sunlight,
they're whistling cherubs
drawing breath from traffic.

They want to be as soft
as pussy willow, the country palm,
white as blackthorn blossom.

They are bleached ears, swollen,
listening to their own crackling.
Logos gone. The waste of lives.

They want to be sprung
from their tetherings
freed from the weight of snowmelt,

these torn pallid rags,
the first white daffodils
flickering along the road's edge.

Other Voices: Tidal Road to Traveller

Now I know why you pressed me to earth,
not to catch blurred stars in my ditches,
but to risk the amphibious edge
where wind shocked oaks turn from the surf
shying from my back of salt bitten pitch,
where your wings of water, your wake of tyres
fling clay and sand at my thorny hedges.
For hours, I stare at weed floating like hair.
Golden mimulus in the freshwater burn
tumbles down to me with its many faced concern.
When the tide undrowns me, I'll sometimes think,
rather than carry you home, I should sink
myself forever, but still I raise my spine to the air,
let the salt and fresh waters stream me bare.

Man Walking

(after Giacometti)

To grow in the shadow of the mountain
makes you take long shadows into your heart.

Three months of darkness in a year, and when
the light comes again, the hikers are small

visions, tall as the gap between finger and thumb,
or tiny men slung in the box of a cable car.

Skiers, the size of toy soldiers, conjure the blank snow.
You want nearness, to hold the intimate eye

with your eye, before the flesh falls away
dissolving to mere structure, the frame of bone.

You'd like to build some large solid figure,
but your tamping tampering fingers, your hands

with their restless palmings and pressings,
pick at plaster, scrape it wet from the maquette,

fidget away excess, leave your prints in whorls
and contours and scraps. Your restless fingers

won't stop till the figures shrink from metres
to centimetres to these matchbox people,

a pocketful of work. Returned to the mountain,
you whittle and gouge and pare

while thin men turn on their bunks, and some walk
out through the opened gates, walk and walk

through the new space they have missed for so long.
While they starved, you starved your figures

to small almost nothings as if you were tuned
to the mad thinning of the world.

You rattle them back to Paris in matchboxes.
And some of your people, though pining, grow tall,

pin waisted and lost in the broken spacious arenas,
grow back like the shadow of the mountain,

hold the mountain's shape between their legs,
while you scrape away at slopes with your fingers

till you have the outline in air. If you could cast
nothing in bronze, you would. That man wants

to stretch his legs and go, but sometimes
he'll be wasted, sunk in the Seine from the night's

handcart of cast off models. Sometimes
he'll survive, bronzed and pockmarked like rock.

Your self-portrait is the dog, louche and loping,
carrying its ragged heart of air between its legs.

Your cat stiffens every liquid move, every pad
and pounce, to the metallic rod of a back.

Your women are as still as pines, ancient as fetishes,
tall as totems or embalmed goddesses.

Little men are busy looking out from raised platforms.
They are the small dark sparks of the almost void

that their size draws around them. And one of them
has managed to stretch himself to a long height,

and is pointing, while another has cast off clothes,
flesh almost, has thinned himself to pure movement.

He's seen something, there in the distance. His heels
drag up the earth, as he strides out, hoping to find it.

Other Voices: Ant to Sky

I am the creature that you cannot tame.
The palm trees of clover swing above me
with the pale watermarks of moths' wings
washed on their leaves, their snapdragon heads
twirled into brown mops, their stems
downy as a woman's skin. I have walked them
both, stem and skin, known them, particle by shed
particle. These are the marathons of my life:
the tall poplars of the summer grass, the pine
bark, ridged and mountainous, the forests of fern.
I tackle the vertigo of dock, lay claim
to those red spires where you lie, clouded, stern,
raining on my many selves as we form lines,
grip dust, dig down among the roots of ling.

The Table

It was the round world of tea.
It had a pedestal foot of mock walnut.
It had been pulled under the bramley
on the lawn which became lawnless
where cow parsley and dock held
the grasses in their sway. It was
a plate of drips from the apple twigs.

Like Hardy's *clocks and carpets and chairs*,
it was out *on the lawn* all day and then for years.
It was a flat world of peeling veneer
near the safe hedge of elders and elms.
It offered nasturtium salads and peppery remarks,
flawed like the internal specking
of the bramleys, with their sepia stains.

Among the campions and apple blossom,
it glowered and mouldered and glowed,
a greening pool in a green light suspended
among nettles, its circle just visible
shadowed by the pink gold towers of dock.
When we slapped down cards, the green world
trembled and wobbled on its carved stem.

I want to lean my head on the ribboning surface,
and ask, Grandad what do you hear?
I want to unfreeze his ear from the trench
and see him listen again to the shelling of beans,
the downy shucks' light fall on the table.
I want the people back who stood between me
and death with their unlocked doors.

Table, float them back to me
up the slope from the stream, through
the hogweed, past the bare bean poles,
till they're back under the bramley with you.
Let your curved drawer stick as it used to,
the handle gripped in their tired hands,
then wrenched open and free.

Kingcups

Some had titles: General, Commander, Major.
They wandered the lanes with labradors.
They wore suits to church and tweeds on walks.

We would spy on them through the weavings
of hedges, through wrought iron scrolls,
through gaps between palings.

I saw him once sitting on a fence, staring
at the kingcups in the ditch. His eyes
were watered blue and red.

He held a buckled leather bag
that clinked, as he drank
to the kingcups' glowing golden faces.

There was the gate to the narrow field
opening between the slopes of two woods.
There were the hollows of chalk diggings.

There were many places for scenic drinking,
for children spying. For that slight limp
and trip, for the hand's tremor.

Once I noticed his frayed cuff,
another time the sun spotted skin.
We pulled wild strawberries

from their star flowered stems.
Creeping thistle leaves brushed
our fingertips with tiny stings.

We cranked the pump's handle
to raise its hoarse gurgle, until he said,
'Be careful. It's condemned.'

He wandered on with his clinking bag.
You thought of them always in a war,
meandering through a map of lanes.

Now, I think of the untitled men,
the plain misters, their heads also
full of fire and burnings,

and how they dug out the leaf drift
with their spades, their hands
wrenching out kingcups, the flowers over,

unblocking the ditch until the flood
retreated from the lane's surface
and slipped back into the stream.

Gifts of the Old Traders

He's packed the gift, rolled it in whale skin, stowed it
in the keel. Ohthere likes the feel of the real,

not the face value of foreign coins, but a silver bowl,
ells of seal hide rope, the shoulder bone of a deer.

The shadow compass guides them to the shore they seek.
They row upriver, a sea monster come inland,

in this new peace of new money, new markets.
In the king's presence, Ohthere's slaves

unroll the present, the tusks of the whale horses,
the North's ivory. And the king knows their future

will be fashioned in the carved covers of the holy books
he orders. Yet the gift he loves best is not these long teeth,

but the words after a jug of wine, the boasted journeys,
the knarr sailing north of Ohthere's home on a whim

to see whether anyone lived there, the crew clinging
to the black ice of the deck with their bared feet,

the meetings with isolate fowlers who bartered in mime,
their only speech rough grunts and shrieks,

the tales of the tusked whale horses hugging
their young on ice floes, the fishermen

cutting holes in the deep white wastes
and then dropping down fishtraps, the snow bears

and their snowy pelts, the flapping lines of drying fish,
the flocks of unnameable birds.

Later Alfred dreams of Ohthere returning to the long house
where he is his own king, falling asleep

on a sack of feathers paid to him in tribute
by the Finns. This is the real gift, Alfred thinks

as his scribe writes it down, this story that will go on
forever now, the ways of the heathen traders,

the fish holes, snow bears, whale horses, greedy fowlers,
on and on, trailing smoke through the days of low light

from small fires kindled on ice, the sparking fat
of the plucked fowl, the cindered bones picked clean.

Grass

The grass speaks, and this is its language:
einkorn, emmer and spelt.

There is the grass, and this is the question:
who knew its first greenness?

Whose fingers lingered over the grass
to gather the seed in the crease of a palm?

Whose children played with the spikelets and glumes,
then ate the small mauve trees in their hands?

And who first ground seed to dust between stones,
packed its flour in a hunter's pouch

then bound it with water, the dough
wound round a stick to cook in the fire?

And who bred the seed, larger and larger,
fed its upright plaits and straw bristling lines?

In the big field at the back, the combine harvester,
like a house lit-up on wheels,

lumbers over the dusky edge of the hill,
and, in the kitchen, you pull out the bread-maker

sift flour through your fingers. Tonight
the meadow grass grows and is needed.

Tonight, the dough swells and then cooks.
No answer but this slice of a field, its stalks,

vetch, daisies, silvering seeds,
feeding the old hungers.

Health and Safety Stops the Raft Race

there will be no more thefts of pallets
from the yard's dump, no more turning of blind eyes,
no more Sundays of hammering oil tins and plastic tanks to planks,
no more nailing bits of two-by-four,
no more paths opened to secret fields behind secret farms,
no more brushed balsam popping seeds,
no more thrown eggs, no more pitched flour,
no more legless plastic seats, no more pink wigs,
no more rugby players in drag, no more paddles,
no more life jackets, no more peering under a low bridge
where the sun spirits jizzling water onto curved brick,
no more loud hailers, no more unroped gates, no more stiles,
no more heavy sodden trainers tracking
the riverbed's shingle isles, no more gliding into the bend's hook
where water deepens to full lakes of cloud,
no more shivering stewards, grappling the wedged rafts,
no more ambulance waiting at the weir's edge,
no more boys quacking at ducks, no more punk rock pirate girls
puzzling near the dam, then choosing the easy way,
hoisting their raft up and over the meadow
and shoving it in again, no more arm chairs
silky and decorous, balanced on water,
no more neighbours partying on the mud bank's brink,
no more corks bumping over stepping stones,
no more tea vans, no more tea,
no more voices floating up to bloom in the branches
of alders and willows and sycamores
murmuring the river's sunken nettled route
to the paddock where walkers and rafters gather,
and where there will be no more dogs,
no more port-a-loos, no more generators,
no more squalling toddlers, no more ice creams, no more trophies
and the deep brown river will stay quiet
and the paddock will sleep like a ward
under a thin green blanket

Against bullet points

- because Christopher's cat and Elizabeth's fishhouses won't fit
- because a girl took time to make a neat blot, then wrote a 'whistling door' but could go no further
- because no one knows how to punctuate them, : ; . – ?
- Because how can *I know what I think before I see what I say*
- because they nudge themselves up power points, click-clicking agreement
- because a woman wrote, 'this house hates secrets' but could go no further
- because they mimic perforations but show no light
- because they bully syntax into pieces
- because they would never extend a metaphor to a friend
- because they are sulkers, asking over and over, 'what's the point?'
- because they are blunt talkers to whom the relative clause is unknown
- because they fence the margin
- drip drip drip into your head
- interrupt before the first word has been said

Our People

There's a painter
who can't stand to see a knife.

She'll turn the blade in under a bowl
of oranges, or paint onions sliced,

the paper skins off in a purple heap,
the bone handle jutting out behind the board.

Her enemies are saws with tiny barbs,
the bread knife with its row of bevelled grins,

cleavers bristling from a cross-hatched block,
or sharpened edges she overshades with blue,

showing only the handles' ridged ebony
or bakelite blistered on a hot ring.

Masonic, we know each other by these clues:
the kitchen's absence of Sabatier, the emptied drawer,

a scythe bound round with rag,
a whetstone buried in the darkest corner of the shed,

or the way we'll use the butter knife
to peel an apple.

Other Voices: Flints at Birling Gap

We are written through you, script everything
in a big rounded hand. We are your ink.
You are our page, our canvas, the blank sheet
we infiltrate with our hardness, our driven words
or clusters of phrases, our chronicles. We think
we support you, line on line of us, grinding
grains of sand revolved, melted, blown like glass.
Vitreous, we think ourselves virtuous, concreted
round with lime, little internal glaciers, stone
that, broken, and chipped heart to heart, can spark
fire for the patient obsessive. Risen through grass
we leave you stumble holes and gaps, our dark
surfaces mimic the cut of diamonds,
scattered in rows, each of us, a sound, a bone.

February Fences

Bracken blows against boundaries
making fences into wind-blown hurdles.
Its copper brightness wraps knots of wire
with weavings, draping frames of air
with patterns and bosses of dried fern.
You think it's safe to cross the wire now
without snag or risk of ripped skin.
But the coverings are stalks, swept
up and over by gales, not safe, not solid
after all, and leaf-mush tamped
in place by snow or driving rain,
stories told over, year after year,
till the frames of mist and mud return,
and the fences, lightened of their drift,
lean over the ditch at the field's edge,
shocked by their own thinness.

Buried Forest

Pepys' friends are digging a dry dock
when their spades slice through tree tops.

Twigs stretch out to mud as if the earth is sky.
There are hazel shells, whole but empty.

In dashes of spanished, frenchy English,
he scratches his shorthand by candlelight:

a woman up against a door, fashionable skirts,
his finger, stained and aching from its labours,

committees and singing in inns, sex and psalms,
blue rolls of wallpaper for the girl he'd made his wife,

and a bluing eye to match the new bedroom.
Open the covers: arms of oak cut into ships,

Mrs Bagwell's *mamelles*, a friend caught on the pot,
green spectacles. Ear to the road:

brush of plague paint reddening a door,
ice cracking on the river, a forest rustling

underfoot in silt, its sighing branches,
the sound of flickering pages, fired

by the whispers of jealous husbands
and wives counting the seconds till morning.

House Arrest

After the gentle switchback
of the escorted drive,
the wide road stretches
down the grid, which shows
the curve of the world
in its misted length
of tailors and dry cleaners,
where Vietnamese girls
bend over sewing machines
taking in seams,
where the Zesty's pizza boy
kneads the dough
and flips it into the air,
where the hardware store
piles boxes on the sidewalk,
where thin women gather
on the stoop gesticulating
and mouthing words
he can only guess at
to the invisible listeners
plugged into their ears,
his car crosses Park Avenue
and takes a street
whose tunnelled awnings
lead up to the yawning doors
and tight faced doormen.
His wife touches his arm.
He walks the marble hallway
to the elevator, glances back
at the rectangle of light,
senses Manahatta moving
on its swamp, the lie of it
shifting under his feet.

The Listener

Foreign voices, those strange 't's,
a murmur that could be grasses
hissing in the wind, the tiptoe of boots,
the brush of cloth on wire,
the tearing of a sleeve. Sometimes
he thinks he hears the whispering rattle
of corn, though it's winter,
and he knows that cannot be.
Wind in the trees could be the sea,
he thinks, as he leans inland
and freezes to the ground.
If he listens hard enough, all the sounds
of the year will play in his head,
gorse seeds popping in heat,
drum skins vibrating,
the trafficking murmur.
His frost-bitten ear, his dry tongue
strain to sort and name each sound
long after the enemy has gone.

It's Not on Google

how he claimed not to know how to eat trout
or how she leaned over and drew the fish bone out,

how he told her he wanted to live in her room, how he loved
the florist's daffodils that she'd shoved

in jars, how heads close, hair electrified, faces pale,
they'd made out the censor's scribble on the torn blue air-mail,

how he'd said, 'they want me to know that they know',
how the town fountains froze into fingers, and how the snow

fell that year until they saw ice form at the river's edge,
and how the daffodils wilted on the window's ledge,

and how he chanced on her so often in the lengthening street
that she changed her way home, fearing the tap of his echoing feet.

How one day, googling, she smiled to think of the trout,
of her friend's quick mind, and the line he'd spun that caught her out.

And it is on Google, how he'd bent his words to a cause
and reeled back into the arms of his young country's laws.

If only she could catch him, freefalling, and carry him back,
show him the eulogies and then rewind, backtrack,

to her terrible laughter that last day under the yew,
where she'd tell him the young rarely know what they do.

Saintes Maries de la Mer

For years, they've talked of the open grave,
the shock of it. Silence might have saved
them from an oarless boat, salt lips
mouthing for food, eyes squinting at each wave.

Three Marys and one Sarah
now float towards this heat.
Their lives are the gasping mackerel
they catch but don't eat.

They, who've known the blade on skin,
can't slit scales beneath gills,
can't even improvise a knife,
can only splash the fish back in.

Words become an undertow of mud,
a quiet wash through sand and root
that clogs their tongues, sponges
scars of leaving. They want this flood

of low lying marsh to heal
the sting of vinegar, to dull
the knock of hammers, to calm
the flash of faces the night unseals.

Palms hardened by driftwood,
the Marys scull through weeds,
weave through flat blue water,
find nests miraged in the reeds.

In the crypt, little fires burn.
Flames in red glass. Bloody capillaries.
Each prayer scorches the air. The years turn
refugees to effigies.

Spring after spring, gypsies lift
Sarah over leather goods and cars,
carry her past the carousels and bars,
honour her to the sea's edge.

All night there's singing in the streets,
the smell of wine, smoke and heat,
the dance's beat breezing out
to girls under drifting tarpaulins.

Music House in New England

Here they leave doors unlocked, whether of porches
with their insect mesh that blurs the sight
of the outdoors to a printed view,
or the back door with its window
to the skeining stream, where frogs
pulse and dive, their emerald heads alert along
the property's unfenced edge.

We see the young oboist swaying
in the lit square of the night.
We hear his notes stretching
and curving out of the window
where my daughter sways to his music
and searches the night sky.

The oboist doesn't know she's there,
a fellow musician of the dark.
He doesn't go with us as we walk
the road, where the white wooden houses
breathe tiger lilies, where we photograph
the stars shooting through puddles,
where the lonely white houses reflect
on the wet surface of the road
the rippled, broken visions of themselves.

Do the frogs hear the music, as the stream
ravels over them? Dogs are curbed by invisible fences
that shock them if they venture over the line.
But the boy's notes fall free as breath
into the unlocked houses. Only the wooden chimes,
moved by the breeze, answer from a tree.

The News from Lake Shaftsbury

There's a canoe hauled up under a stone pine,
on the lake's island. The beached prow is a sign

of children who paid at the State Park Concession.
They've left paddles, life jackets, some confession

of escape, yellow clues to a scene,
cast off near the gunnera, shadowing the green

water. They must have floated over furred weeds,
thin blue fish jiggling away towards reeds.

Maybe their soles stepped softly, but frogs still leapt
in springing arcs from the trickling edge and kept

on jumping in, in almost succession. Now damselflies flit
through the gnatted air. A pine cone rolls. Slips

of shingle make eddies sway the moored boats.
Life jackets alchemise water to gold. A dog lopes

on the slipway. Light cloud on the mountain, a blue
patch of sky. This too can be news:

the drift of their shimmer, a returning canoe.

Isolation

You called it 'the cell', the room where
the radiator ticked and grew cold.
A cell to wait in while cells died. The choice,
a knife, a pill or liquid from a bottle of lead,
like the last choice in a fairytale,
where the wrong choice could leave you dead.

Once, afterwards, there was no room, no cell,
and they trolleyed you into a corridor's gap,
tickertaped you with yellow and black,
and there you were lying on your back,
between the loos and the kitchens,
seeing out your radioactive hours
by the flapping of the swing doors where,
from the stench, I would guess the drains
had blocked or overflowed.

You were seeing out your hours,
on a trolley next to a trolley of dirty plates,
that were piled high and rolled and slopped
near your head but placed on the other side
of the tape as if air and a plastic strip
could save passers-by from radioactive you.
And they let me sit nearby
on a sateened sofa next to a standard lamp.
The sofa floated in front of the gouged
out wall. Strange war zone. And yet,
though they'd parked you in a corridor of junk
as if you were junk, you were absorbing the gamma rays,
and your tumour stopped for a few months.
It was not the nothing it seemed
as I sat there against the broken plaster
and watched you, eyes flickering at the trays
going past, at the clumsy manoeuvres
of dressing-gowned men.

Yes, it meant a few months more
and, floating by the gouged out wall,
on the boat of the sateened sofa,
I felt a strange hope rise in me
even when the kitchen doors
bashed the wall, even when
a nurse placed a tray on your head,
confusing your bed with the trolley.
Even then.

the memory of the heart

you're out early   the blue cotton smells clean
there's mist in the gorge   an edge of steam

you're the lens of a hand-held camera
uneven as breath   you're the flash of a blue chimera

a glimpse of speed   as you cross the wired-up bridge
the tidal mud   the stone ridge   over and on to the downs

socks yellow with pollen   you pound grass
you pass the concrete cathedral   a drift of mass

georgian terraces   where seagulls taunt
their squall rising   you're haunted

by a woman on the news   today   the law will kill
her with a needle   run faster faster to the snuff mill

past the ruins of the gas works
catch the stench of blubber boiled for oil

condemned arches   cyanide in bricks
you think of that woman again   lick

your upper lip   sweat pouring now along the docks
past galleons used for films   the mock-up quay

your ankle gives on a sudden dip of stone
worn by bare purchased soles   chained bones

but quick here come your mates   arms strong   thighs lean
dark wet backs longboats jerk along your eye's spool

roofed by rusted bikes   half-painted gypsy buckets
at the warehouse boiler suited men have found a locket

you pass them tweezering the grass   ticker-taped
where yesterday you ran watching the blue shoulders

of your friends   shrugging uphill to your door
where your girlfriend served you all *café direct* in blue mugs

and you sat on bath stone steps   five blue runners
hamstrings stretched   wringing out the good sweat

and you are you and him, me and you,
I am your new muscle, pounding you up lanes,

moving you, you who would sit static for hours
this is my beat, and his, in you

I am your new muscle   shifting your legs, your view
memory transplanted   me in him in you

From memory

Their long rounds –
the gins, stouts, bitters, barley wines,
twenty or thirty drinks
that they'd recite –
a litany of celebration.

'Read us the menu, my darling.'

Just the sound
of a word or number –
that's all they needed
to know the price and name
of everything forever.

They mocked my slow totting up,
then paid with wads and wads of notes,
big gold flashing from their fingers.

Beer flowed from the pump,
and cash flowed as if
the pickers were millionaires,
slow handclapping a clown,
who took to walking
the floor's length at closing time
on his hop torn hands.

At night they'd shut their eyes
to lines of poles and bines.

Now the pub is smokeless,
well behaved. Above the bar,
a swathe of dried hops
rustles and whispers,
pulls me back to those

blue slant shadows
that used to stripe the field.

I stand in the empty pub,
listening for the order,
the sing-song chant,
rhythmic as an auctioneer's,
questioning my own thirst
and the words I read, hear.

Caravan Man

Lanes lifted him – and trees too.
Fields sang him to sleep,
moated him with ditches,
walked him through the day.

Gnats that could hardly
stay on the ground sought him
though cars veered round him,
a charcoal smudge on their screens.

The gassy kettle, the mug
and the sliced bread
all knew him well
on those mornings

when the grey sky blanked itself
against the may hedge. Drink
heated his lips, scorched
his throat. Furrowed earth

formed itself into shoes
around his shoes, softening,
heavying his steps. He was not
daunted by the early birds

or the wind and thunder
which spooked horses
on wild purpling evenings.
But people daunted him

with their soft hellos,
and then their hardening eyes
that fell to the ground
so often that he searched

for those glass marbles
through nettle, dock
and balsam, rolling them
in his hand and mind

to find the image
of that blown moment.

Three seed heads introduce

their friends, a couple
of long spoons in a window,

a pair of skinny lovers.
What use are they?

Strange dancers, retired now,
half-starved. The sill is

their wooden bed
where they lie

under the watery sun.
Soon a person will come

and take them to feed
someone old,

who can only be fed
the tiniest soupçons

of the soup's
dipped bread.

predator

a barn owl came through my window and pecked open my head,
tore out with his claws the story that was growing there,
covered in grey fur, wet and blind, where its mother's tongue
hadn't yet licked the vernex off or the eyes open,
and he clutched it and flew up into the night thermals
taunting me with long vowels and cries to his girlfriend –
he fancied himself as a wit – I saw him in the sprayed field
flapping slowly away, his wings creaking folded paper,
the story torn yet still stirring

The Truth

The house was open – that was the truth
he'd swear to always. The table
was already broken. And a bird,
a swift maybe, arrowed under the stone
lintel, its song a small screech.

The scribbled mess the bird made
on the Afghan rug, lying on the stone
flags of the house, was the truth.
As was the song on the radio
that crackled from the kitchen table.

And it was the truth when he said
he tiptoed into the house, tripped
on the upturned table, followed the bird
up the stone steps to the room where
another song boomed on a bass line.

The house was open – that was the truth
he'd swear to always. The bird was sent
so that he'd find the stone, that had landed
by the bed and somehow chipped the table.
He never heard the real song of that house,

the voices that cried out, excited,
'Look, there's a bird.' Voices that made her
lay her pencil down on the music table
with the song half formed in her throat.
Voices that cried, 'Look there's a stone.'

The Rave Murals at Racton Tower

Cave painters left the images of their eyes
        bulls and calves, swimmers
like sperm muscling through rock,
        dolphins racing, a shock
of deerhounds or lurchers
        leaping to a hunter's cries.

Then the brushing of egg white
        on walls, gods eating for the last time,
the tempera drying fast,
        no one knowing it would last
so long in the soul's eye. Now lime
        softens to a knife at night.

And there's the scratch of a name on a wall,
        signing a forever on the space
between the ivy and the empty frame.
        Maybe it's a game,
which will resurrect a face,
        a name – at least until the brick falls.

Spray-paint can reconstruct your face,
        your grass stained band,
deliver them in red or blue,
        give you that eerie rave space
of the head, that touch of a trembling hand
        the making of a presence, a clue.

A stick in ash draws back to the folly
        the lighters of fire-pits, figures
who ache to be known
        or owned
in a tower, empty of eyes, of stairs,
        smoky dancers shadowed by holly.

Racton Voices

tower to air
You knew me first when I was rising, bare.
You climb my sills where nettles sway.
Often you've tried to hide in my hollowness –
you are the well of my empty stair,
the breath of a father who will say
to his son, *I am the nest that is swallowless.*

ivy to tower
I start at your foot. I know you can hear
my sap rising round you. I want to stretch
myself up to your height, pace myself out
hand over hand, as if I am my own rope.
I run clear of the dock, outclimb the vetch.
Listen to my voice rustle in your empty ear.

tower to boy
You've woken after the noise of the night
bones aching from the cold, fingers numbed to blue,
face all new stubble, lungs furred by smoke.
What happened here lit by the fire-pit's flame
in this unfinished alcove?

ivy to tower
I cling to your edges. I clothe your flint skin.
I bud on you, flower. Birds spread me about.
I pity your fixedness, watching me frame
arches and windows among the trees.

tower to boy
                              It's true, like you
I'm an empty room, not yet made good, soaked
by rain, misunderstood. You finger tubes, the residue
of fireworks, the mattress' frame. Left behind,

you trace your words on my brick, the flicker of a line,
a clue, some sign you want someone to find.

ivy to tower
I put my gloss on everything, the sheer
drop, the runnel of mud, the path to the sea.

tower to boy
You could stay here all day, watching the light
play its refracted games on my crumbling walls,
but the ivy's roped a trail back through the trees.

tower to ivy
A mother's nails, blunted by brick,
unsucker you from me, uncover a name.

The Blue Den

He can choose from several horizons.
The electricity lines. The sea.

This is him now.
A bunch of old doors for walls.

A knocker, like a shrunken head,
nailed to the one door that opens.

He's painted all the doors blue with the old paint
he found, the day the girls turned from him.

The sea scuds through the pallets.
The wind rattles the blue tarpaulin.

At night, behind the dredged doors,
his skull fills with the sea's battering.

If anyone should wash up here, they'll know
the territory by the ragged flags.

His blue coat flaps up the shingle.
He has become the flag of his own outpost,

a blur almost merging with the cloud.
He wants to be to the air, what the seal is to the water.

A drop of deeper, darker blue, a patch of stone,
of weed, a camouflaged shadow.

It's harder to fade into the sky than into the sea,
however many blue coats he puts on.

Winter sill

Who opened this window
on to the snow?

Who let the north wind blow
the frail curtains to one side?

Who placed on this icy sill
two spindly hyacinths,

green stalks splayed apart,
whose single separate stars

stare out at the starred dark?
Who angled the bowl to catch

the gleam of a small moon
from the far sky? And who

asked the night to come down
to the dripping trees to slip

under their charcoal shade?
And where is the frame?

The pane? The latch?
Have they dissolved in the cold?

Answer me that.

Gathering a still life for the sill

Though the fields and hills swerve away
from you like some contour map
who juggles you in its valleys,
you drive down unsurfaced roads
careering on cambers, about to fall off,
feeling the lack of edges, until
you're past the wild bamboo in the ditch.

You lurch off the lane into this:
a field of tall heads, stalks blackening
in heat, huge periscopes all fixed
in the same direction. Your head
is level with these big heads,
their roundness crammed with seeds,
their dark suns flickering with faded
flames. You take the veg knife
from the cubby hole of the car
and cut the fibrous stems, collect
a bunch of the heavy heads,
gathering your harvest before the seeds
go to the yellowhammers, before
the oil is pressed.

Back home you find the striped jug
and see the stems swivel. You fear
the heads will throw their weight about,
that the last jug he made will topple
and break. You cut a wedge from the melon's
marbled green. The pips in their nest
of pale orange flesh shock you. The figs
you scatter along the window's edge
grow sticky and yellow. In a few days,
you'll hang the sunflowers upside down
from the eaves, hoping the yellowhammers

will cast the seed to the winds, that yellow
will come back to the sunflower fields,
where the tanks lost themselves,
where long ago he dived for cover,
where the stems are still burnt charcoal,
look like black lamps or shower heads,
wait in ranks, keeping each other upright,
wanting the energy to follow the sun.

Wilcoxes, December 2010

Secateurs find out
the jasmine's weavings,
its specks of gold
in freezing fog,
its artist's tangle
dark against the wall
it needs to nest on.

Easy to cut long stems
of shooting stars
before they reach
the earth, take root.
Easy to say you care,
to take them in,
though you may
guess the heavens
will come to this:
sharp, cold metal,
sap's quick reversals,
twigs upended
in a winter's vase.

At Washington Zoo

I think of this story: an orangutan meets a man
beside a river. He holds out his hand. The man takes it.
They stand. The orangutan's calm eyes,
his stillness mesmerise the man. They stand for hours.
The man not daring to move. And when he tries,
the orangutan holds his hand more firmly. They are
stuck in this gesture that has come through centuries,
an offer not to draw the sword, whether you have a sword or not,
a touch that joins right hand to right hand,
palm to palm, fingers and thumb holding each other.
Somewhere a fire rages, or a bridge is breaking,
invisibly and slowly as a river rises.
Or there are bandits burning a village.
I can't remember which disaster plays
out ahead of the man. The man holds his nerve,
lets go of pulling away and instead considers
the orangutan's brown eyes, as Christopher Smart
considered his cat Jeoffry. The man notices
the ape's long arms, feels the muscular power
reaching back from his palm, meditates
on the orange hair, the tousled head. The man
with his hand in the orangutan's hand
has been standing in this poem a while now
while I watch an orangutan swing along
parallel ropes between towers at Washington Zoo.
When the orangutan lets go for no
reason that the man can see, the man shakes
with relief. He starts to walk forward and
a mile on sees the bridge broken in two,
the fire raging, the bandits leaving, the water
subsiding. He can feel the orangutan's hand
still, the tough palm, the rough hair of his arm.
He has tuned in to the intense listening. He has
watched the calm eyes. He thinks of his father, once

when sadness and madness had entered the house,
when shouting raged from the rooms,
and crockery and knives and ropes
had taken on random lives of their own,
his hand on his arm, saying, 'wait, son, wait'.
And how they had stood outside together,
his father holding his hand, their breathing
calm and synchronised for a long long time,
until the noise subsided. Later when we try
to sleep in the spare room in the suburbs,
these men of the forest come to me, loping
along vines, knuckles down, gathering branches
to build beds in the canopy. Through this haunting,
we turn and sweat in the heat, hearing the fall
of each hickory nut from the garden tree.

Other Voices: Fallen House to Final Owner

You're here again. Now I've dissolved,
broken on the beach, like memory, like water
coming inland from the heat of the world.

Though you don't see me, I'm with you
in the undertow, in that washed splinter
of blue paint that drifts in the shallows.

Though I'm all to pieces, I'm here
in the brick ball shifting under your feet,
in the wisp of nylon, its mesh of air

caught on a rock, in that tongue of leather
drowned on the day she cast her shoes
over the edge, boats sailing a choppy surface.

Remember the wasps that stung the nape
of her neck? Remember the nest I grew
in the rafters? Its huge head layered with paper?

A home that you speared with a pole,
lobbed into the sea, its lantern globe
blotting up the tide, then drowning.

I thought I was married to the cliff.
I thought the horizon was drawn
to my line of vision.

You think I can't taste but I felt comfrey
flower in my mouth. I pulled inside
the blossoming currant.

I thought the petrels were calling me,
the gulls were my friends, that the clean mint
by the door grew for me.

You need me now that your mind
is a worn cliff, a rattle of pebbles,
your view unseen steps climbing the air.

To see her, you'll need
to dredge for battens, to sift through sand
for shatterings. Shake off the beach

and gather me up: hearths, lintels, stairs.
Oil the iron latch of the bedroom door
that stuck over time. Rebuild the sill.

Hang the nets in the window,
where she stood naked, the sash rattling,
her blurred hair full of static.

Pile the driftwood in the grate. Strike
the match for the kindling. Undrown
the songs she sang. Let my salt walls

flicker the light back to you – and there
she'll be, on an afternoon of thunder,
the lines of her body uneroded, clear.

Shore me up this time. The sea is rising
to the rain's thin needles. Keep me here.
Then I'll keep you where you want to be.

The flood houses

Through your window, the houses
across the road cluster together.

The road is a moving tidal sill
of water that raises its silt

until these houses cross the view
of tarmac, mud and river,

then climb through your window,
shouldering each other out of the way.

Look. They have knocked over your daffodils
and broken your earthenware jar.

They try your interior and then your view.
But see only themselves looking back,

peering at the wild bunches settled
on the sills of their own drowned windows.

Oriel window

Wine dark dahlias
in a turquoise vase
in the window
over the bay
correspond
with the one
red light
of the single
fishing boat
returned
for the night.

The red curve is
a Japanese stroke
on the dark blue sea.

What is being said
by colour
that we cannot say?

Storm and the tea cup

You cannot tame the cliffs easily
into a background of white chalk.

You cannot hold the sea in the lens
of a wooden casement

or swivel a tornado
in the cup left on the sill.

You can only show this:
the storm framed by a square,

the curtains whipping away,
the sky bold and blued,

the driftwood on the sill
unsure whether to drift

off through the unlatched window
and eddy out into the water

whose scuds of foam are blowing
in now that the sea is calling

for its scallops and conches
and filling the fortune-teller's cup

with the salt of its tide.

Cloud window

Net curtains fog at the edges.
There was a dog, that much
memory will tell you still. A view
of a lane of grey stone and fuchsia.
Beyond the frame, lines of hills,
an estuary, burrows of sand
with shacks that peered up
from tracks trailing to the distance.
There was mizzle, then hard rain.
There were pylons, trying
to break through. There was
the faint outline of a penciled gate.
There were rocks mapped
by lichen. There was the strange
grey green palette of the sea
on an out of season afternoon.
There was someone with you,
with a face like the mist hovering
at the sill. There was drizzle,
then a name, then clouds, like these,
coming in through your window.

Repossession

None of it fits on the sill:
the bailiff's keys, his cell phone,
his bulldog neck and neat case,
the lawyer's brief, the deeds.
Maybe these small pebbles,
this fossil, these marram reeds
you stuck in a jar? Or this drift wood,
these scallop shells? This conch?
You slip them into your pockets
as you climb over the sill's edge.
In the harbour, you lay them out
on the mean tide line, returning
what you owe after all.

Pipe

This is the mouth of the pipe
that pushed its head through the ground,
yet was wrenched from the spring.

This is the tough metal trunk,
armless and legless, found
alone outside the city wall.

This is the water carrier,
Aquarius, propped on rock,
arc shadowed, a round shade.

This is the screw unscrewed,
the bolt unbolted, the river
dammed, diverted.

This is the parched mouth,
the tea unminted, the water unboiled,
the dripping tap solved.

Flash light falls on this relic,
the god of baths and jugs,
whose unplugging makes mud.

This is the head scarved by threads
gathering thoughts for the walk
over the lost foundations.

This grey pipe, unchanneled,
unscrewed from a cistern,
or torn from an underground system,

surfaces, a find on a dig,
a fragment quietly
transferred to plinth and paper.

View from the basement

Bars, leaves, a ladder to the light.
Some women's shoes, their straps
tight over the ankle bone. Someone's
lace-ups, a man's trousers, the ends
worn into heel catching loops.

This is not your artist's dream
of a high room of glass with a view
over the bay, a single palm in a pot
and the green of umbrella trees.

Instead you rip off your clothes
in the underground heat,
paint these arrows of women,
their dark triangles of hair,
their heads like knives.
Then when they're dry,
you hide them beneath
a dust sheet, terrified
of what you've done.

Coming round in the room above,
you need your still lives still.
So you place a melon, a newspaper
and your own head twisted away
on the window sill, then stand back
and squint at these double
selves talking over the world.

Free style

I come home from work on the second day back.
The word *value* has been on everyone's lips,
while the month has been saying goodbye
to heat and blue skies with blue skies and heat.
There's a message on the phone, and so I drop my books,
hurry down to the field where the picnic, half-eaten,
is spilt over the rug, and the cold bags lie open and where
the river has cut through the sandstone's gold rust,
and sheep's hooves have made small mountain passes,
winding along the steep banks. Down in the water
my friend is swimming, the sand clouds behind her.
Her daughter is swimming too. And the dog is swimming,
a wet dab of black under the willow's floating wool.
It is September's last day for wild swimming,
the gnats and flies treading air over mud and dung.
My friend's daughter, who is also my friend, has come
home to us. She has come back. Her long hair streams in the water,
going with the flow of the river's weed. And I think how swimming
is like reading, or surviving, and how it's possible to slip back
into the river's writing, into the current's flow, and how,
when the weeds backstroke through the water,
they look up through the alders and willows to the sky,
become green rippling lines, intuitive, inevitable
as you hope the lingering trout will be.

bargain

tip of finger to nail of thumb,
numb skin to metallic eye,
sigh of silk and cut of thread,
tread of feet and cup of hip

gleam of glass and plastic beads,
seeds of light, flash of glitter,
flitter of lids on tired faces,
traces of sweat on a wild seam

raw cotton, picked, unpicked

Variations on a plain hem

I am reading a book on sewing
on the plane from New York,
high in the sky at night rising
above its light map, then sea,
reading about converting fulness
to ease, with little irons or darts.

I learn that two people will press
the same cloth differently,
that hems can be felled,
blindstitched, stabstitched,
that a hem can be overcast
or bound by a strip of bias,
that sometimes all you need
are running stitches,
long and easy as feet
loping around the park.

It's all about not showing where
blades cut or rip through the bolt,
about making fast any loose strands
which could unravel later.

All around, zigzagged hems,
slipstitched hems complete the clothes
of air travellers, who sleep blanketed,
or read under dimmed lights,
their ears headphoned to music.

I think of the fingers,
perhaps of children, who rolled
those hems, or the seamstress,
the machinist in China or India,

or the mother at her kitchen table
hiding the raw edge in a fold.

Here, in the body of the plane,
we touch the brush of their backstitch,
the traces of their DNA,
the whorl of each finger,
flying with us through the night.

Doves nesting in a palm tree

Out of the window's sight:

two thin cats roam
under the orange tree
that drops fruit to the ground.

In sight:

a dove flies from the nest
of its tree at the sound
of the long hinges

swinging open the shutters
to the balcony. Back and forth,
back and forth, the mother dove goes.

Two fledglings preen themselves.
Their world from egg to being
has been one long sway

in this palm tree, and they think
the world sways and their tree
is still. Soon they'll leave

this view of wavering windows
and quavering roofs.
No room for fear under this sun.

Two cats prowling.
Three doves on the balcony.
View of an empty tree.

Anguis Fragilis

A slow worm lives for twenty years or more.
This slow worm existed before
my children were born, my parents died.

The slow worm, no blindworm, watches
the changes in this garden. Seven years for the wild,
that was already taking hold, to take hold.

Mistaken snake, narrow legless lizard,
it bends its way through the poppy stalks
where huge red heads weigh them down,

petals opened to the charcoaled stamens.
It has lurked under the fuchsias,
slithered over matted alpines.

The slow worm knows what I know,
has slid under windows, heard the noise of words,
trusted the garden with its young –

those small flickerings,
silver gold esses, Saxon smith work,
that I almost killed for baby vipers

the day I unlayered the drive
from its thin new covering
of earth. The slow worm

is as slow as a poem's growth,
winding over the tarmac,
long witness to the wilding.

living fossil

in the sprayed field – sand –
striped red – manilla – maroon –
   ochre grasses and

at the edge –

fresh green – the bristles
   of the horsetails – surviving
fire – arthropods – ice –

Rabbit in Leamington

I'm coming into Leamington Spa station,
when I remember a past self
watching a rabbit here years ago.

Something terrible had happened
not long before. Yes, the bad
and often threatened thing had happened

or nearly happened according to the letter
that came through our door. It was a cold night.
It was raw. A man battered the phone box.

'Get out you bitch,' and words that were harder
and more violent, not to be recorded here.
'I'm phoning a hospital,' I shouted.

And my boyfriend put his arms around me
and blocked the opening door with his back.
And still the drunk kept hammering,

shouting he needed to phone a hospital too.
It was months later, the warm dusk of a day
that I watched the rabbit, nibbling at grass

on the verge of the station garden.
The lights were coming on in Leamington
and I couldn't get the tramp

out of my mind or the frozen panes
of the phone box or the smell of piss –
even though there were petunias

now with their sweet bought scent.
Somehow the rabbit was the tramp
the tramp the rabbit, but the good boyfriend

was still the good boyfriend
holding the heavy door shut,
and I thought of him at home

in his garden, gently preparing a rabbit,
undoing its skin with a knife
and turning it inside out

like a jumper pulled off the body
until only the head was left,
stuck in the knitted neck,

and the way he missed his lab
and drove me back on the icy roads
to whatever would be waiting there.

Portsmouth Valentine

Napoleon and Nelson left
women at home to manage or mope.
But Emma danced naked on tables,
and Josephine didn't wash.

I stretch out across the bed,
can sleep landscape if I wish.

In dreams, I am eating soap,
or clearing the deck of spoons,
when I hear your key in the lock,
the ghost of you home
before the ship even docks.

Recovery

She was stepping over blue broken china surfacing
from the earth's garden, searching for the green rose
of a cabbage, its purple rivers, its stored drops of water.

She edged past bare bean poles and crouched
as her cat crouched, thinking his head under cabbages
made him invisible. And she felt invisible too.

The slugs nurtured in the cabbage's folds could be her friends,
and so she unstuck them, placed them on the path,
where they fed microbes with their silver flow.

Then she cut through the woody fibrous stem,
and the cabbage rolled in her hands, a smile of leaves,
a globe of green, blue whorled, misted and mauved.

She forgot herself that day, marvelling at the way
she shared the DNA of the sap with the snapping jaws
of the caterpillar whose lace work she would discard,

losing herself in there somewhere, as she followed
the fanning paths of the inner unpeeled leaves,
to the lightening, lightened heart of the world.

The Green Mile

(after Peter Lanyon)

What is the green mile?
  It begins with houses,
hydrangeas, stone walls,
    mats of thyme.

Where does it lead?
  To a hole through a cliff
with handholds of rope,
    where you glimpse

through the rock, your friend
    swimming, hair red against
the blue tide, where you hear
    the buoy like a night-jar

warning of outcrops
    so that hikers stop
at the eerie sound.
    Then the green mile changes.

The day changes.
  Now it's tall vegetation,
the heat of foxgloves, campions,
    cowdung on trainers,

stone hedges,
    sheepsbit, coltsfoot,
flies, humid ferns
    you could drown in.

What is the green mile?
  A baby in a backpack
wearing a sun hat,
    a miracle of sleep.

It's the stream soaking the hill,
    water rushing to more water,
the wooden bridge,
    the calm words of a stranger.

It's the sunken lane to the farm,
    tyres weighing down hay,
eggs for sale,
    an old tin box.

It's the clouds' shadows,
    boulders of sky shifting
over fields that fall back
    from cliff paths.

What is the green mile?
    The sea staining the rocks,
white heads of hogweed in grass,
    the froth of surf,

dark hunches of gorse,
    stone stiles, sprays
of montbretia in rain,
    silver lichen

or maps of rust on headlands
    we thought were always ahead,
but here we are, walking the green mile
    with its stonecrop and bugle,

the fuchsia growing wild,
    the curves of the current,
abstracted below us,
    then suddenly there beside.

When you are under

drink the rain. See through the bars of the drain
the river you've made of the road.

When you are under,
when the car jolts to a start, then tears you over tarmac
till you're an oily cut-out, a pressed overall,
when your back is bruised, your lungs full of brake fluid,
when the silencer bounces on your chest,
when the hard shoulder gives you the cold shoulder,
stare at the undercarriage. Memorise every bolt.

When you are under, watch yellow ripple
overhead as skips of waste float downriver,
their yellow progress waggish, sassy, like yellow wagtails
that flirt and skitter on the shale beach of your tidal river.

When you are under,
in that moment before the crane lets slip the city's detritus,
compressed cubes, wrappers, designs for millions of eyes,
inhale the chemical reek of old print, meat rot. Here it comes:
gaze up to the top of your crater. The big jaw opens.
Now swallow the discarding of the day. Then eat your way
towards roots and grass, the undergrowth.

Long for the wild saplings to feed you and feed on you.

When you're under the pier,
peer up through the weed greening the pilasters,
through the linocut of girders. Count
how many soles appear to shutter your sky.

Remember the men who went under.
Cooks stewing plums. Midshipmen playing backgammon.
Their linstocks, lions, griffins, alligators,

hung above the hammocks, carved from boredom and lulls.
Knees of trees in the hulls. Silt half the timbers,
then let the rest ghost away.

Even when you are under,
you'll sometimes find yourself in fragments,
like this Roman stone in the honeycombed road,
where your view is an iron rim hooped to wheels
trapped in the rut they made of you. Misshape metal.
Throw your sparks out into the air.

Then it may be quiet for years
while a shoot creeps over you and into the groove,
until the bindweed flowers, unfurls
its trumpets, turns its many faces up to the sun.